DATE DUE			
MAY 0 5			
DEC 5			
JAN 3 1			

LOOKING
FORWARD
TO A
CAREER

Writing

ETHEL ERKKILA TIGUE

dP

DILLON PRESS, INC./Minneapolis, Minnesota

8283

©1970 by Dillon Press, Inc. **All rights reserved**
Second Edition 1976

Dillon Press, Inc., 500 South Third Street
Minneapolis, Minnesota 55415

Printed in the United States of America

Library of Congress Cataloging in Publication Data

Tigue, Ethel Erkkila.
  Writing.

  (Looking forward to a career)
  SUMMARY: Advice to writers on self discipline, writing,
and selling manuscripts. Includes information on careers open
to writers.
  1. Authorship—Juvenile literature. [1. Authorship. 2. Vo-
cational guidance]   I. Title.
PN151.T5   1976   808'.025'023   76-6536
ISBN 0-87518-131-7

Contents

ACKNOWLEDGMENTS

Collier-Macmillan, *The Modern Stylists,* Donald Hall, ed., by permission, the quotation from Ezra Pound. Crowell-Collier, *The Writer Observed,* Harvey Breit, ed., by permission, quotations from Truman Capote and Henry Green. E. P. Dutton and Company, *On Creative Writing,* Paul Engle, ed., quotation from Paul Engle. *The Horn Book Magazine,* June 1968, quotation from Edward Fenton, by permission. Rand McNally and Company, *Counterpoint,* Roy Newquist, ed., by permission, quotation from Maurice Edelman. *Saint Paul Pioneer Press-Dispatch,* permission to quote John H. Sorrells. Ruth Slonim, author of *San Francisco: The City in Verse. The Writer Magazine* for permission to quote B. J. Chute, Margaret Cousins, Frances Shields, Norma R. Youngberg, and for permission to adapt material from "Don't Wait to Write Your Novel" by Ethel Erkkila Tigue, an article which appeared in September 1963. *The Writer's Digest,* by permission, quotations from Geraldine Rhoads, Erskine Caldwell, and Alma Boice Holland.

The photographs are reproduced through the courtesy of Honeywell, Inc., p. 55; Minnesota Department of Natural Resources, 17; *New York Times,* 51; Palmer Writers School, pp. 29, 41, 91; Poetry Society of America, p. 75; U. S. Air Force, p. 58; and the U. S. Navy, p. 63.

Introduction

"Words can kill and words can make alive."
—Norma R. Youngberg

Sooner or later every young writer hears this warning: Beware of clichés. Good advice! Clichés are those worn-out, ready-made expressions that often point out the lazy thinker, and one thing a writer must not be is a lazy or a fuzzy thinker. A writer must find more original expressions than "good as gold," "balmy breezes," or "live and learn."

Once in a while a cliché can be helpful because a cliché states a familiar truth that needs no explaining. For instance, this one: *It takes all kinds.* This cliché can serve as an introduction to careers in writing. It does indeed take all kinds of writers to fill the writing needs of our nation—and other nations of the world.

Never before in our history has language, both written and spoken, been so important to the survival of the human race; never has communication been so instant, so global, so varied. There are thousands of newspapers; countless magazines, books, pamplets; endless television and radio programs—and all of these depend on words, words, *WORDS!*

Where do all these words come from?

Somebody writes them, of course. Most of us take it for granted that newspapers are written by reporters, and that magazines and books have authors. We are less likely to remember, however, that almost every word spoken on television and radio was first written down by someone: playwrights and scriptwriters wrote the stories, advertising copy writers wrote the commercials, journalists collected and wrote the news broadcasts. Every word in print—whether it appears in a school text, in a notice to the PTA, as a blurb on the cover of a music album, or on a piece of direct mail advertising—every word was written by a writer of some kind.

To learn more about writers, let us visit Mr. Frank Charney's seventh grade English class at Woodson Junior High School. Mr. Charney is one of those enthusiastic teachers who can make the dullest lesson interesting. His students are seldom absent—they are afraid they will miss something. Mr. Charney's fame began the day he stood on his head for five minutes in front of his class to demonstrate a yoga posture.

One Monday morning last winter his second-period English class entered his room to discover their teacher, with a bright red tam tilted over his dark hair, writing on the blackboard with a piece of chalk to which was attached an enormous ostrich feather plume. When the bell had rung, he strode to the front of the room and announced: "For the next two weeks we are all going to be writers!"

Noises of delight and moans of pain came from the class. Then one bright-faced girl in a front seat giggled and said, "I thought it was artists who wore tams—not writers."

Mr. Charney tickled her nose with the tip of the feather. "Correct! Writing *is* an art. Writing is an art, a craft, a profession, a job, a career."

"But I thought writers are supposed to be born and not made," said the girl. "How can you make us all into writers?"

"Not correct this time, Jane. Writers are born, made, trained, educated—and pasted together. Some are geniuses, some are craftsmen, some are good, some are bad, and some are average—just as you students will be in this class."

"What are we going to write about?" a boy shouted from the back of the room.

"Good question. Your first assignment is simple: Write about anything."

"Hey, that is hard," the boy protested. "Aren't you even going to tell us *what* to write?"

Mr. Charney shook his head. "Not this time. The first lesson a writer has to learn is the lesson of self-discipline." He turned and wrote "self-discipline" on the blackboard. "Self-discipline means that *you* make yourself do what needs to be done. That *you* are the boss. No one forces you or pushes you, but you make yourself do it. Any professional writer will tell you that discipline is as important as talent."

"Can we write a short story?"

He nodded. "Fiction is fine. Let your imagination go."

"Does it *have* to be a short story?"

"Of course not. It can be anything." He turned once more to the board and wrote:

"Out of yourself create . . . Look for your own. Do not do what someone else could do as well as you. Do not say, do not write what someone else could say or write as well as you . . . but out of yourself create . . ."

He read it out loud. "A great French writer by the name of André Gide said that. Those may not be his exact words but I think you understand what he meant."

A big boy sitting near the window let out a loud groan. "I don't know what to write about."

Mr. Charney asked, "Craig, what do you like to do best?"

Craig smiled and said, "Play baseball." The class laughed.

"What position?"

"Catcher."

"How does it feel to be behind that catcher's mask when a good fastball comes zinging at you? Or a wicked curve that takes off?"

Craig's frown disappeared. "Well, it depends. If there is a runner on third and . . ."

Mr. Charney interrupted. "Do you think you could describe what it feels like to be a catcher in a very important game where two teams are tied for first place?"

A big smile lit up Craig's face. "Sure! I could write that. I didn't know that's what you meant."

Mr. Charney pointed with the ostrich feather to the

words on the board. "That is exactly what those words mean. Write about what you know better than someone else."

A hand went up in the middle row. "Could I tell how my uncle is making a color television set from one of those kits you can order?"

"Making a color television set!" several voices echoed.

"Does he expect it to work? Hey, I would like to know about that!"

"Looks as though you have a good subject, Kevin. An author once said that a writer is a person looking for an audience. It seems as though you have yours. Your article would be a somewhat technical article. Be sure you have all your facts straight. That is especially important in a technical article."

The clown of the class blurted out: "I want to write some of those funny commercials for television. Like that icky flu bug with the big sticky feet tramping around in someone's stomach."

The class laughed again. Someone yelled, "Out of yourself create, Chimp!"

Without realizing it, Mr. Charney's class was separating itself into some of the writing categories that this book will discuss in the following chapters: the short story writer, novelist, non-fiction writer, technical and business writer, journalist, advertising copy writer, and several others. Mr. Charney was also suggesting some things that writers need to know in order to be successful in their chosen fields.

As the class ended, Mr. Charney gave his would-be authors this bit of parting advice: "Think of your writing as a trip. You have a starting point and you have a place you are heading for. Decide both before you begin to write. Then take these steps." He wrote them on the board.

    1. Think it through
    2. Feel it through
    3. Write it through

"Today we have been working on this first step—thinking about what we are going to write. The clearer your thinking, the better your writing will be. The second step is especially important for those of you who are going to write fiction. Try to feel the way your characters would feel, try to put yourself in their shoes. During these first two steps, you can make notes or an outline. But the actual writing—that is the very last thing you do."

What do the writers in Mr. Charney's class have in common with the career writers whose work will be described in following chapters?

Both groups of writers must choose the type of writing they can do best. Both must try to make words serve a particular purpose. Both must learn the discipline that gets writing done. (It is much easier to *talk* writing than to *write* writing!) Both groups must think, feel, write—and then rewrite—to make their ideas come alive to their readers.

Career writers have an additional problem.

They must find a place to sell their work. They must find a "market" for their words. Newspapers, magazines, publishing houses, industry—these are the writers' markets, the places waiting to buy their word-products. Marketing is one of the most difficult parts of a writing career.

There are two kinds of writers marketing their wares. One type—reporters, editors, and advertising copy writers—sell writing services directly to an employer and work on a salary basis. The other kind is called a "free-lance" writer. Such writers—the short story writer, the novelist, and the article writer—work for themselves and sell what they write wherever they find a market for it.

The next chapter will tell about the different kinds of markets where both of these types of writers can sell what they write.

Supermarket for Words

"Whether a writer likes it or not — he's in business."
—Alma Boice Holland

THIS LITTLE PIGGY went to market. To the literary market, that is.

Would you believe a forty-eight page, monthly magazine devoted entirely to pigs and hogs? That is exactly what *The National Hog Farmer* is. You ask: How could anyone possibly fill an entire magazine month after month with information about pigs? What would there be to say about them? Here are some of the topics covered in one issue: "People Pose Greatest Threat of Foreign Disease [to livestock]," "New Antibiotics Improve Gains," "Blood Dysentery Hits Iowa Herds," and "Time for Action on Hog Cholera."

Magazines like *The National Hog Farmer* are known as *trade journals*. These are publications that serve one particular industry or trade. There are several thousand such trade journals in the United States. Just to give you an idea of the variety, here are a few such magazines: *Bakers Weekly, Space Age News, Midwestern Druggist, Playthings* (for toy stores!), *Petroleum Today, Pump Digest,* and *Rubber World.* Trade journals buy about five thousand articles each month. One successful trade writer quipped, "I make my living by writing for magazines you never even heard of."

Somewhat similar to trade journals are the publications known as *house organs.* About six thousand house organs are published by large companies and distributed to their employees, stockholders, and sometimes to their customers. Contents usually cover such things as information about company activities, ways to help employees and employers to get along better together, and stories about the people who work for the particular company or industry. House organs are usually "staff written," which means that the company hires its own editor and perhaps a writer or two for the job. Lately, however, there has been a trend toward buying more material from free-lance writers.

The magazines most people are familiar with are known as *consumer magazines.* The consumer is *you,* the general public. These are the magazines you are most likely to find on your coffee table at home, such as *TV Guide, National Geographic, Time, Family Circle, Reader's Digest,* and *Sports Illustrated.* These periodicals employ some staff writers (people who write for that magazine alone and work on a salary) but also buy a great deal of free-lance material. Articles must be well written, well researched, and of current interest. The standards are high, but so are the rewards. An author can make hundreds of dollars for an article in the very top markets.

Fiction for these publications also brings high prices

—several hundred dollars or more for a short story. When beginning writers send a story to one of these top magazines, however, they must remember that they are competing with the best writers in the country.

Other magazines which use both fiction and nonfiction are the mystery, confession, science fiction, children's, and religious magazines. Their payment to writers varies from one cent to ten cents a word, depending on many things such as length, quality of writing, name of the author, and the needs of the magazine.

The most familiar publications are the daily and weekly newspapers. The *World Almanac* lists more than 1,800 dailies and 8,800 weeklies.

It is easy to take our newspapers for granted—they appear on our doorstep or porch without fanfare. But just stop to think of the number of words required every single day to fill all those newspaper columns, including the advertising areas. Thousands of people are busy day and night just to get the nation's newspapers printed.

Newspapers need many kinds of individuals who have ability with words and language: reporters, editors, proofreaders, copy readers and copy writers, columnists, and advertising sales people. Most newspaper writers are salaried; they work directly for the newspaper on an hourly-wage basis. Newspaper editors also do buy some free-lance material, usually features and special stories.

Some five hundred radio and television stations spill out words in as great a flood as the newspapers, and their needs for writers are quite similar. Writers are in demand in the entertainment, news, and advertising departments. The constant cry here is for something new—and writers must pick their brains and talents to provide it.

An expanding market for writers is the *book publishing* field. Some 3,500 book publishers put out more than twenty thousand new books a year. Paperback books are selling as never before. Many paperbacks are reprints of hardcover books, but there are also many originals.

In spite of the growing market, getting a book published is not easy. With the costs of making books increasing every year, publishers must be careful in their choice of manuscripts. A book must not only be well written, but the publisher must believe that it will sell well.

Consider that it costs a publisher quite a lot of money to publish and sell a first novel. If the novel sells only fairly well, or poorly, the pubisher may not get this money back. Of course, if the company is lucky enough to have a bestseller on its list, it may not matter too much if another book is a loss. Most first novels do not make money for a publisher, but the publisher is gambling on the writer—not just on his or her first book.

The book publishing field also provides jobs for writers in advertising, publicity, reading of in-coming manuscripts, editing of manuscripts that have been purchased, proofreading, copy reading, and writing blurbs for book jackets.

More and more writers are finding their place in modern business and industry. Here writers work in advertising, public relations, sales promotion, production of manuals and training guides, writing new-product information, and as speech writers for top executives who make many public appearances. Thousands of writers are employed by some four thousand advertising agencies and publicity firms.

All levels of government—city, county, state, and federal—require writers for much the same purposes as does business. Cities, counties, and states need writers to create good publicity stories, to research historical brochures, and to make up promotional material to encourage tourists. Top government officials on all levels need speech writers, and legislators and legislative committees cannot function without researchers.

The federal government alone publishes hundreds of booklets, which are sold by the U.S. Government Printing Office. A look at some of their titles suggests the wide variety of these booklets: "Narcotics and Drug Abuse," "Pruning Ornamental Shrubs and Vines," "Driver," and "High Blood Pressure." The United States Information Office (which explains America to other countries of the world) employs a large number of writers. Writing positions in government are filled either by political appointment or by civil service examination.

Right about now you must be wondering: If there are all these markets to write for, all these places to send one's stories and articles to, how can a writer possibly decide the best place to send his or her work?

That is a hard question to answer. Many writers, especially beginners, are stumped by it. Getting his or her work to the right market is a constant problem for a writer. Even an eager reader cannot read all the magazines and books to find out what editors want. Besides, editors change, policies shift at magazines, some publi-

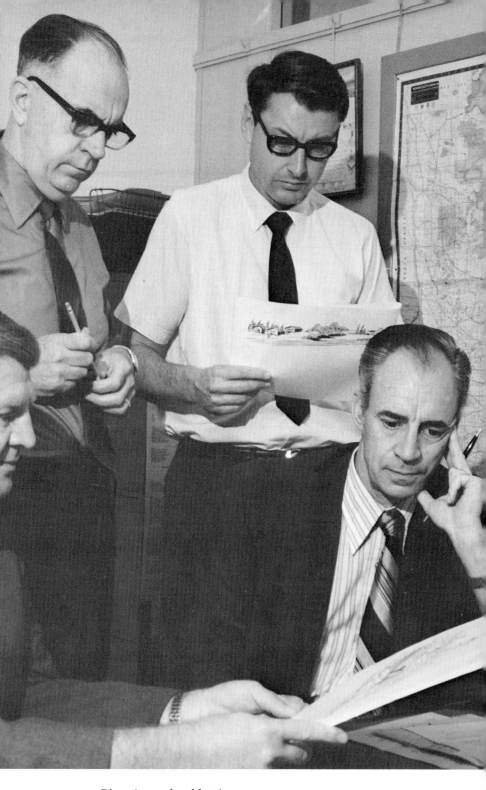

Planning a booklet for a government agency.

cations go out of business, and new ones appear on the scene.

There are two books which are of great help to writers. These books are *The Writer's Market* and *The Literary Market Place*. Each one lists all possible markets, the names of editors, the needs of the publications, desired lengths, and rates of payment. Also helpful are the writers' magazines, which carry monthly listings of editorial needs.

Many professional writers work through a *literary agent*. A literary agent is a market specialist whose job is to sell writing: short stories, articles, plays, and books. Agents usually live in New York, the publishing center of the United States. There they can keep tab on what editors are looking for, and they know where they can get the best deal for their authors. As an agent's authors succeed, so does the agent, since an agent works for a straight 10 percent commission on all he or she sells. This means that an agent wants writers whose work is salable. He or she rarely takes on an unpublished writer. Therefore, beginning writers must, as a rule, struggle along by themselves, sending their work to whatever market seems best for them. When they have had some of their writing published, an agent may be more willing to gamble his or her time on their work.

This chapter has described some of the many opportunities for writers. Following chapters will tell more about the special needs of different fields and about some of the tools that are necessary for success.

Just what are a writer's tools?

A typewriter? Yes. The ability to type is certainly

important. Pencils, pens, erasers. Mailing envelopes. Stamps. You will need all of these. You will also need a good dictionary and a thesaurus. (When you have a word and want its correct meaning, you use a dictionary. When you have a meaning—such as, "a sort of reddish color"—and you want a specific word for it, you use a thesaurus. Under "red" you would find a long listing: ruddy, scarlet, blood-colored, sanguine, flaming, salmon, rosy, pink, cerise, claret-colored— and many, many more, suggesting all shades of "reddish" color.)

More tools: Paper. Stacks of paper. Yellow for first, second, and umpteenth revisions. Carbon paper for copies. Good white paper for that important final draft. Is that it?

Not by a long shot! This list leaves out the most important tool of all. What is that?

The next chapter will tell you.

Which Window? What View?

". . . it is only what we respond to with a leap of the mind and soul that we can write about with any conviction."
—Frances Shields

THE WRITER IS THE MOST important tool of all.

Everything about the writer affects his or her work. The writer is like a giant filter through which the raw material of life must pass before it can be put into words on paper. The writer's total self will determine *what* he or she chooses to write about, *how* he or she writes, and how deep and honest his or her insights are.

How, for instance, did John Steinbeck, the Nobel Prize Winner of 1962, decide to write about the wandering Oklahoma farm workers in his famous novel, *The Grapes of Wrath?* And about the Mexican and foreign laborers in his book *Tortilla Flat?*

Mr. Steinbeck knew his material well. He had labored in the large fruit and produce fields of California, he had been a seaman on a Panama freight boat, and he had worked as a ranch hand and a carpenter's helper.

Through his own experience and observation he had gained an understanding of what it meant to be poor.

Would he have chosen to write about poor people if he had never shared any of the hardship? Probably not. What he had personally known and seen had given him a special "window."

Each writer has his or her own "window on the world." One can experience only part of life—not all of life. One's writing is influenced by the family one was born into, by friends, education, and by the books one reads. One's senses are important, too. It has been said that your writing is no better than your observation. How good are your eyes? How sharp your ears? How sensitive your nose?

Physical health affects writing. Are you healthy, do you see life as exciting and challenging? An outsider who thinks that writing is an easy job may ask, "What effort does it take to just sit in one place and pound a typewriter?" A great deal of effort, any writer will reply. Energy is essential to good work.

Emotions greatly affect writing. Emotions are what a writer feels—not what he or she thinks. How does a writer feel about people, about politics, about race, religion, and family members? All this will influence his or her work. That is why ten people can write a story on the same event and none of the stories will be the same. Each author will be looking through his or her own window and seeing his or her own special view.

Poet and novelist Paul Engle, in his book *On Creative Writing,* probably said it as well as anyone: "The first and most important point about writing is that there is no such thing as material itself, apart from the way a person sees it, feels toward it, and is able to give it organized form and expression in words."

Suppose a high, old house had three windows—one in the basement, another window on the first floor, and a third one in the attic—all facing the same street. Would the view be the same from each window? Of course not. The person looking from the basement might see nothing but grass and sidewalk, legs and feet, tires and wheels going by. The first-floor observer would have a broad, detailed on-the-level view of all the people and activity on the street; while the one in the attic, glancing down on the passerby, might miss some of the details below, but he or she would have a beautiful view of the sweep of sky and distant horizons.

A private window on life: that is one kind of viewpoint. It is the built-in viewpoint that is part of each writer (and each person), whether he or she is aware of it or not.

There is also another kind of viewpoint that is equally important. This, however, is a viewpoint which the author chooses. It is the point of view from which he or she decides to write a story or article. To understand this other kind of viewpoint, imagine the following situation.

Peter, who was just sixteen last week, passed his driver's test on his birthday, and now, two days later, he has the chance to take out the family car alone for the first time. Because he is so proud of his new license, he plans to drive up and down the neighborhood so his friends can see him behind the wheel of a new car.

Two blocks from the driveway where Peter is turning onto the street, Mr. Smith, a police officer, is sitting in his patrol car. Recently the police have been having trouble with teenagers in this area. Mr. Smith has also been having some trouble at home with his own seventeen-year-old son. Right now, sitting in the patrol car, he is recalling an unpleasant incident that happened at the breakfast table that morning. All of a sudden he becomes aware of the fact that a new white car with a teenager at the wheel has circled the block two times. He decides to follow the car.

A block away, another young man is coming out of a house carrying several rags and a can of car wax. For the second time that week he is going to wax his Model-T, which is parked on the street.

Just as he is coming down the sidewalk from his house, Peter spies a classmate at the corner of the block. He lets up on the gas pedal and rolls down the window so that he can call to her as he cruises by in the new car.

And then it happens! Peter has not been watching, but he catches the form of the Model-T out of the corner of his eye. He jams his foot on the brake! It is too late—he hears a metallic crunch.

Now suppose you were a writer and wanted to write this situation into a story. The first thing you would have to decide is from which person's viewpoint you would tell the story. Remember that when you choose a viewpoint character, it is through this person's eyes and ears and feelings and thoughts that the story is told. The choice of a viewpoint character will actually determine much of the story itself.

How many possible viewpoints are there in this situation?

Peter's, of course. He seems to be the main character. A writer could choose to use Peter in "first person"—

that is, as the "I" telling the story. The writer might begin something like this: "The accident happened the first time I took the car out alone."

Or the writer could use Peter in "third person," beginning: "Peter grasped the steering wheel tightly, and a sense of power passed through his fingers as he turned the new white car onto the tree-lined avenue." The story would be about Peter, but Peter would not be telling it directly.

Or perhaps the author would decide to use the police officer's point of view. This would make an entirely different story. What kind of a man was Mr. Smith? How did he feel about teenagers in general? Would he carry his grudge against his son toward another boy of the same age?

Or the writer could use the young man with the Model-T as the main viewpoint character. Here again, a different story would emerge from the same situation. How did he react when he saw what happened?

And there are still other possible points of view: Perhaps a spectator, such as Peter's friend standing at the corner. Would she be sad, glad, or indifferent to Peter's problem? Would she know the other young man?

A neighbor out mowing his lawn might tell the police officer what he saw. He would use an "objective" viewpoint—that is, he would not show any particular person's feeling or thoughts. He would try to tell what happened just as accurately and factually as possible. Again, the "objective" viewpoint would create a story quite different from the others.

Do you see now why the choice of a viewpoint is so important for a writer to make *before* he or she begins to write?

In summary: This chapter has touched on two kinds of viewpoint. One which is a part of the writer, a part of his or her built-in experience and not a matter of choice; the other viewpoint is all a matter of choice—it is the writer's selection of the best focus from which to write the story he or she wants to tell.

The next chapter will discuss, among other things, how short story writers learn to use both of these kinds of viewpoint in their work.

A Career of Storytelling

"I think that people cannot live without stories any more than they can live without bread. I think there will always be fiction."
—Margaret Cousins

IN LONDON IN 1897, a lively Mark Twain read newspaper reports that he had died. This prompted his famous cablegram to the Associated Press in New York:

THE NEWS OF MY DEATH HAS BEEN
GREATLY EXAGGERATED

Perhaps the same may be said of the short story.

For years the death bells have been tolling for the short story. Critics have predicted over and over again that the short story was on its last legs, that the real world was so much more exciting than the world of fiction that people no longer needed stories. Editors began to fill their pages with articles, leaving only a token spot for the world of the imagination. One large Sunday magazine supplement cut out all fiction from its pages—only to be flooded with so many protesting letters and telephone calls that the publishers were forced to change their policy—and to bring back short stories and novels.

Fiction was not dead after all!

When asked whether she would continue using short stories, editor Geraldine Rhoads (who has worked with *McCall's, Ladies' Home Journal* and, at this time, was with *Woman's Day* magazine) stated in the *Writer's Digest:* "I've always believed that the short story, like a parable, may be the very best way to say something to a reader, and I don't think we can afford to drop any means of communication as effective as fiction."

But we may as well recognize that to be a short story writer today is much more difficult than it was a generation ago. Only a handful of successful writers make a living at it. Most short story writers also write nonfiction or novels, or have other jobs.

What makes it so difficult now?

One simple fact: fewer short stories are being printed. A magazine which might publish one story today would have published several about twenty years ago. Some editors say that writers themselves should share some of the blame, that editors would use more stories if writers sent them better manuscripts. But writers must eat. So they write that which is most likely to sell: the article.

Stories themselves have changed. They are harder to write. Today's readers are better educated, more sophisticated, better informed, and more critical. They no longer accept the "good guys-bad guys" formula for fiction. They demand a greater honesty. They know people are not all-good or all-bad, that a hero is not 100-percent hero. A hero or heroine may have a streak of weakness that makes him or her more human, more like the reader.

More and more conflict in modern stories takes place inside the characters. Writers need to look into themselves, to know themselves, so that they may know others. Writers need to understand that what they see through their "window on the world" is the true source of their material.

Nor is the story itself a neat package the way it used to be with a definite beginning, middle, and end—with all the strings tied neatly together, all the questions answered.

Boy meets girl. Does boy like girl? Does girl like boy? Does boy get girl? After some complications, yes, yes, yes! And they live happily ever after.

Not in today's short fiction.

Today's short story may ask more questions than it tries to answer. Or it may leave the reader without any answer at all—letting him or her determine what the answer is, if there is any. Some people dislike this kind of modern story. One woman said angrily, "I am tired of finishing stories for writers! I wish they would write stories with real endings, the way they used to." But the modern short story often seems to say: This is the way life was for these characters at this moment of their lives—do their experiences have any meaning for you (the reader)?

Not all stories are like this, of course. Mystery stories, suspense stories, and children's stories still depend a great deal on "what happens next" rather than what

A free-lance writer at work.

happens inside a character. These stories are full of action, events, excitement, and movement. And there is demand for these kinds of stories in particular types of magazines.

Confession magazines are the largest market for short stories today. But their stories also have changed. Once they were known as "sin and suffer" stories. Today, they deal with modern subjects and are written in a more modern, realistic style. Confessions still use the first person viewpoint: the "I" tells the story.

Short stories in religious magazines are not necessarily religious, nor are they "preachy." They are usually well-written stories that do not disagree with the beliefs of a particular religion. Editors of religious magazines are often very helpful to a promising beginner. Although their rates are not the highest, the work of many excellent writers appears in these publications.

So far, the discussion has been mainly about the "commercial" short story—the story which a writer *sells* to a consumer magazine. Other publications, known as literary journals, reviews, or "little magazines," also use short fiction. These publications, usually put out by universities or colleges, are the market for the *literary* short story. A literary story is of very high quality, it can be experimental in style and subject matter, and it is written more to satisfy the writer than to fit an editor's idea of what readers would like to read.

Although the payment at these literary magazines may be very small, or nothing at all, the editors of quality consumer magazines watch their pages for new writers. Stories from these publications often appear in collections such as *The Best Short Stories of 1975* or *The O. Henry Prize Stories.*

With all this change, are there then no rules for writing the short story?

No hard and fast ones. Each writer works out his or her own problem. Author Truman Capote has said that "finding the right form for your story is simply to realize the most *natural* way of telling the story."

But these suggestions might help a beginner:

Use just one viewpoint in a short story. Only a very skillful writer can successfully switch viewpoints and get away with it. A beginning writer does well to stick to one point of view. This makes the story stronger by giving it unity. For instance, in the Peter incident, a writer would not jump from Peter's feelings into the police officer's mind and then into the other young man's thoughts—not without creating a hodgepodge. The reader would not know whose story it was.

Choose a small block of time. Time to a writer is like a piece of canvas to a painter. For a short story choose a small canvas. A short story does not try to cover a lifetime; rather, it is a segment of life, a high point of experience in a character's existence. The writer is looking, as though through a spyglass, at a particular person at a particular moment.

Shirley Jackson, the noted short story writer, gave this recipe for the short story: use three incidents, one minor, one slightly less minor, and one major.

Start your story where the action is (on page 1—not on page 4). As one author put it: "Get the cat up in the tree on the first page—then spend the next five pages getting him down."

The Novelist at Work

Forget the short stuff, Sinclair Lewis once advised a small group of writers. Write a book — become known as "the author of."

THE DAY FRANK CHARNEY'S English class began studying the novel, their classroom received an unexpected decorator's touch. In front, covering the blackboards, were hung two full-size patchwork quilts. One was complicated in design and intricately beautiful with rows of multi-pointed stars. Each diamond-shaped point was a different hue of orange, yellow, or red printed material. These stars were then combined with triangles of varying shades of dark green to form a circular design, which was placed on a white square. These squares, carefully hand-sewn together, formed the quilt. Pinned on one corner was a State Fair Blue Ribbon Award.

The other quilt was of random patchwork with scraps of many shapes and sizes sewed together without any real pattern at all. The only suggestion of design was a flowing sense of color formed by the lighter patches being grouped through the center of the quilt, with the sides gradually darkening to deep blues and purples along the edges.

Kevin, the comic spirit who was always late to class, came bounding into the room, saw the quilts and slid to a whistling stop. "Good grief, Mr. Charney," he exclaimed. "I forgot to bring my sewing basket!"

He got his reward of loud laughter from the class. Mr. Charney's eyes twinkled. "No, you did not forget, Kevin," he said. "It is right there—on top of your neck." The class hooted. Mr. Charney added, "All the needle and thread you will need today is inside that handsome skull of yours."

The bell rang.

Mr. Charney stood up behind his desk. He held a medium-sized book up over his head. "This is a novel," he said. "It is a very solid object. Good hard covers. Sturdy binding. It is very real." He brought the book down to shoulder level, opened it, and flipped the pages. "Twenty-two chapters, a total of 285 pages filled with rows and rows of words, one following the other. When you start reading this book, as we will today, you will expect these rows of words to make some sort of sense as you go from page to page. You will expect to discover a story that will interest you and events that will have some meaning. You will expect to find some characters in the book that you will like or dislike, admire, or maybe not care about at all. You will expect all this for one reason: because this is a finished product, a published novel." He put the book on his desk. "But what was this book like to the author when she first started thinking about writing it?"

After a rather long silence, a girl said, "There were

not any words, I suppose—maybe just an idea."

Mr. Charney nodded. "You are right, Sandy. There were no written words." Then he picked up a rather large manila-covered package. "This is what the book was like to begin with. This is a ream of typing paper —five hundred sheets—all empty—not a word on any of them. This is what a novel is like to the writer when he or she begins. The writer has the task of filling all these empty sheets with words."

Kevin raised his hand, then tapped his head with his forefinger. "My sewing basket here cannot figure out what all that has to do with a couple of patchwork quilts."

The teacher grinned. "I was waiting for someone to get curious enough to ask. Well, I will tell you.

"My grandmother is not a great reader of books. But she is a creative person. She creates quilts. She designs them, she plans the colors, she cuts the pieces, she sews them together into a work of art. You see two of her creations hung up here in the front of the room."

Mr. Charney paused. "Kevin's frown tells me his sewing basket still does not get the connection. Well, I didn't either until one day last year when my grandmother was working on this award-winner in our living room. She had the pieces of these yellows, reds, and oranges in three separate piles, these vari-colored greens in another, and then these white squares in a fifth pile. She was painstakingly matching colors for each square to create just the kind of effect she wanted.

"A friend of mine, who was just starting to write a novel, had stopped in, and we were sitting—not far from my grandmother—discussing his book. My friend was talking about all the notes he had been making for this book over a number of years—notes about theme, about characters that would be in the book, descriptions of background, parts of the plot—and how he was now trying to put them together. I remember he said, 'Writing a novel is really a gathering up of things—you gather all these bits of thoughts, some on paper, some in your mind, and then finally you have to sort them out, to rearrange them, and fit them all into a pattern that will hold together and make some sense to the reader.'

"At that moment, my grandmother spoke up. 'That is just like making a quilt,' she said.

"My friend looked at her, rather startled, then he laughed out loud. 'You know, you are right! That is exactly what it is like. You are doing just now the very thing I have been doing all this past week—trying to make some sort of pattern out of all my little pieces . . .'

"I got to thinking about it later and decided my grandmother had made a very good comparison. A novelist does start with bits and pieces that might not even seem to belong together at first—like the pieces in these quilts, this one from an old dress, another from a shirt or a blouse. The novelist fits the fragments together, sees their relationship to each other, and if there is no relationship, he or she throws the pieces away. In the end, the whole creation holds together—the way this book holds together, the way these quilts hold together. For only that which is necessary to the design has been put into each one.

"Some novels are like this first quilt. As you read them, you sense a very definite pattern, you can see how the plot was worked out, you can almost see the design in the mind of the 'quilt maker.' Other books are like this second quilt. You do not see any real planned design at all, but the pieces flow together—maybe the novel's theme, or the background, or a character gives it unity." He stopped a moment. "Which of these quilts would a detective novel be like?"

"The first one!" Craig answered quickly. "I read a lot of detective books. They are like a puzzle. Every piece has to fit in the right place when you reach the end."

"That is right. But all novels do not have that strict a pattern. Many modern novels seem to be almost without any design at all. It depends on the author—what he or she has decided to do with the bits and pieces. The author makes these decisions before beginning to write."

Mr. Charney was correct. A novelist has certain decisions to make before he or she begins to fill those empty sheets of paper. Let us look at two of the most important decisions.

A decision about time. A novel is not like a painting that you can see in one glance. A novel happens in time. Like a piece of music that goes from one note to the next, a novel goes from one word to another. Someone has said that there is a clock ticking in every novel. The novelist must decide how long that clock will tick. Should it tick for the lifetime of the main character? Should it tick for ten years? Or a week? You remember that a short story usually covers a short period of time, a fragment of life. Time in a novel can be *more* than a lifetime—it can cover several hundred years or several generations.

One author tells of starting a book and deciding to make the story cover a period of twenty-five years—

from birth to adulthood of the main character. When he wrote the second draft of his book, he decided that twenty-five years was too long a time, so he cut out the childhood of the main character and made the book happen in ten years. He did not like that either! So he rewrote the book once more. This time the action of the entire book happened in one weekend!

A decision about viewpoint. Here we go again on viewpoint! Unlike the short story, which generally uses one viewpoint character, a novel can have several viewpoint characters. This kind of technique is called *multiple, third-person viewpoint,* or sometimes "bouncing" viewpoint (it bounces from one character to another). Usually the viewpoint of one person is kept throughout one entire chapter.

It is better not to have too many viewpoints, even in a novel. Four or five are enough. One amateur writer wondered why his first novel was turned down cold by editors. A writing teacher offered to read it. She quickly found out what was wrong: He had switched the viewpoint twenty-six times in the first chapter—jumping from this character's mind to that character's thoughts and then into another's and another's—and back again! The result: complete confusion!

Of course, if the novel is written in first person (the "I" telling the story), then it would have a single viewpoint, just as in a short story.

Are you wondering if it takes a special kind of person to be a novelist?

Yes, it does. Special in certain ways.

A novelist must be a person who can bear to postpone success. It takes most writers at least two or three years to write an adult novel, sometimes five years—or even twenty! A well-known successful short story writer says that she has started fifteen novels—and finished none of them. Many a beginning writer also gives up. That is why there are hundreds of unfinished novels in the desks and dresser drawers of would-be novelists.

A novelist must be able to work in a kind of chaos. Writing is not a very orderly process. All those "quilt pieces" have to be fitted into the design, often by much trial and error. No one can hurry the growth of a novel. A novel is like a tree; it grows slowly month by month. A novelist needs patience.

A novelist must be willing to put a lot of effort into an unguaranteed project. Suppose no one will publish the work when it is finished? The novelist cannot think about this. He or she has to keep on working, keep on writing!

Although this chapter has talked mostly about the novel, much of what has been said can apply to the writing of other kinds of books—biographies, histories, and general nonfiction books. All require much thought, careful planning, effort, and often lots of research.

When a publishing house accepts a book, it will buy the book outright for a lump sum, or pay the author an advance against royalties—this may be several hundred dollars or in the thousands, depending on the type of book and the name of the author. A royalty is the money that the author receives from each copy of the book that is sold, usually 10 percent. He or she will also share in "subsidiary" rights, such as movie or television rights, or foreign publication.

After a book is published, the publisher sends complimentary (free, that is) copies to newspapers and magazines for review purposes. Reviews are written by people other than the author and give the reviewer's opinion of the book. Unfortunately, all books do not get widely reviewed because of limited space in newspapers and magazines. A newspaper may receive as many as five hundred books a month to review—and have space to review from twenty to a hundred a month. Good reviews (and sometimes bad ones!) help the sale of a book. So do advertising, autographing parties, and public appearances by the author on television or at club meetings. All these help—but none can guarantee a bestseller.

How does a bestseller happen?

No one seems to know for sure.

If we did, said one publisher, we would certainly use the formula. We would have a book on the bestseller list every week!

The Broad Field of Nonfiction

"Good writers are those who keep the language efficient. That is to say, keep it accurate, keep it clear."

—Ezra Pound

NONFICTION. ISN'T THAT a peculiar term to describe a kind of prose? It does not tell you what the writing *is*—rather it tells you what the writing *is not*. It is not fiction. This is like saying that a human being is a non-horse, or that a horse is a non-human. Not a very satisfactory state of description, but as no better word seems to be available, *non-fiction* it must remain!

Nonfiction is where the writing action is today. One editor called it the "art form of our times." A good nonfiction writer can make an excellent living, and even average writers can find markets to which they can sell. Every kind of publication you can think of is on the lookout for more and better articles. Compared to fiction, articles are selling about nine to one.

Because nonfiction is such a broad field of writing, there are many possible writing careers involved. This

This writer edits what he writes to "keep the language efficient."

chapter will deal with free-lance article writing, and the next three will cover special fields of nonfiction, such as journalism, copy writing, trade and technical writing, educational, financial, and political writing.

This chapter's general information on article writing can apply, however, to the following three chapters, for they deal with special kinds of articles. Whether the articles appear in an educational journal, a trade magazine, or in a political pamphlet, the same basic standards apply.

Nonfiction deals largely with facts, not with the imagination. Nonfiction writers are collectors and organizers of facts. They must be able to interpret the facts they find—to see a fresh approach to the subject they are writing about in the mass of information they have collected. When they present the facts in an article, they can and do use their imagination. More and more article writers are using the dramatic methods of fiction to give zest to their writing. One writer calls this "the fiction of nonfiction." Let us see how it is done.

Suppose you decide you would like to write an article on the advantages (or disadvantages) of early dating. Where would you find your facts? There are several sources.

Observation. Look around you. How many of your friends are dating? How many are not? Are they happy in their situation?

Personal Experience. What is your own situation (if you are old enough)? Has it been what you would like it to be? Do you feel left out? Or let in?

Interviews. Talk to other young teens. What do boys

think about dating? What do girls think? Interview two or three couples who date, and several people who do not. Interview parents about their attitudes.

Research. Use the library—magazines and books. Are there any statistics on dating among junior high students? What do psychologists think about this practice? Does early dating lead to early marriage?

Conclusions. What does all your research show? Does it give you a new slant for an article? Does it, perhaps, suggest an article entitled "Early Dating—It's *Not* Smart!" Or does it suggest rather an article called "Early Dating—Join the Junior Jet-set!"?

Sometimes an author may start researching an article with one particular slant in mind, but change the approach completely when all the facts are in. The viewpoint in nonfiction writing is objective; that is, the writer should be as open-minded as possible. The opposite of an objective article is an article called a "think piece" or a "personal article." This is written in the first-person and expresses very definite opinions. Such an article might be entitled "I Do Not Believe in Early Dating." This would be a personal opinion—usually backed up with research and facts.

After an article writer has collected information from all possible sources, he or she must organize this material so that all the facts flow easily and naturally to the conclusion. How does one do this without boring the reader?

First of all, the writer must "hook" the reader by composing a lead (a first sentence or paragraph) that is so interesting that the reader simply cannot stop reading. The importance of the lead of an article cannot be overemphasized.

One author tells of an experienced writer who was newly hired by the magazine he also wrote for. The two of them were to share the same office. This new man was given an assignment by the editor to write an important article that was to be due a week later. For four days the new writer researched and interviewed. Then he came into the office, put some paper into his typewriter and just sat there staring at it, hour after hour, not typing a single word. When this had gone on for almost a full day, the older writer began to get nervous. At this rate, the article would never be written before the deadline.

Finally he asked what the trouble was. "Oh, nothing is the trouble," the space-staring writer assured him. "It just takes me a little while to get my lead sentence just right. But once I get that, the rest goes easy."

And that is exactly what happened. About an hour later, the new writer pounced on his typewriter and pounded furiously for a few minutes, then leaned back and smiled. "I got it," he said. "Now it will be smooth sailing." From that moment on, the keys galloped over the white sheets, and the article was finished the next day—nicely ahead of deadline.

Here are a few sample leads from published articles. Do they grab your interest?

"Nothing in football history can match the game between Cumberland University and Georgia Tech at Atlanta, Georgia, on Oct. 7, 1916. The score was Tech 222, Cumberland 0." ("The Funniest Football Game Ever Played," *Reader's Digest,* October 1955.)

"I've invented a fabulous new diet. It costs only $2,000 for each pound you lose." ("What a Way to Lose 110 lbs.!", *Ladies Home Journal,* March 1969.)

" 'They're not going to shoot Santa Claus,' said an official of Gump's department store in San Francisco in the midst of the Christmas buying rush." ("Santa the Supersalesman," *Time,* January 5, 1976.)

Once the lead has been written, then comes the organization of the body of the article. A reciting of statistics and drab facts would make dull reading indeed, so an article writer uses imagination to perk up the information. This may be done by—

Anecdotes. These are short little stories told to illustrate a point. The incident about the new writer and his lead sentence is an anecdote. So are the incidents that happen in Mr. Frank Charney's English class.

Quotations. These are usually from authorities on the subject of the article, such as doctors, specialists, or people who were interviewed. An example is the quote from Truman Capote in chapter 4 when he said the right way to tell a story is the most *natural* way.

Description. Vivid images help make facts or information interesting. Examples in this book are the description of the patchwork quilts hanging in the front of the classroom, and the description of Mr. Charney in his tam and with his ostrich feather plume.

Study a few published articles. You will find that each successful piece will have (1) a good lead, (2) anecdotes, (3) quotations or dialogue, (4) description, (5) transitions (sentences between anecdotes or scenes that keep an article moving from one kind of information to another), and (6) a satisfying conclusion that pulls it all together and ties in with that good lead. Many a professional writer will say that you must have *all* these elements in your article if you expect to sell. Do not leave out even one element, they warn.

Selling the article is quite different from selling the short story. Editors of nonfiction prefer seeing a query rather than seeing the entire finished manuscript.

What is a query?

It is a letter written to an editor asking (or querying) if he or she would be interested in a particular article you have in mind. Editors are busy people. Manuscripts pile up fast, but a well-written query can be read in a few minutes.

A query letter should be brief (usually one page), but it should be precise and present a sparkling description of the article and its slant. It can also include some data about the author's qualifications for writing this particular article, especially if it is a specialized field. Be sure to enclose a stamped, self-addressed envelope with your query.

An editor may reject the idea or ask you to send in the article. This means, "Go ahead. We would like to see this article when it is finished. But we cannot say definitely that we will buy it."

They may buy it. They may not. But if the editor has given you some suggestions on how to write the article, the chances are good that it will be accepted. If not, you query another editor.

If they do buy it, you whoop it up for joy! For one article can open the editorial door to others, or even bring a special assignment.

Oh Joy! A Check Every Payday

". . . the newspaper is more than a business or a trade or a profession; it's a way of life."
—John H. Sorrells

AFTER TALKING ABOUT the uncertainties of free-lance writing for several chapters, it is good to switch to a field that provides writers with a good living—and a check every payday! Writers in both the editorial (news) department and the advertising department of a newspaper work on a salary basis, and the work pays well. The hours are good, the working conditions favorable.

When he was executive editor of the Scripps-Howard newspapers, John Sorrells wrote a letter to a young man who was considering journalism as a career. His words are still true today.

Mr. Sorrells pointed out in this letter that anyone interested in a real career in newspaper work ought to consider the role that a newspaper plays in a community. He said, newspapers unite and give direction to a community, they stir things up when necessary (they *can* and *do* fight City Hall!), they point out needs, they express wants, they give a community knowledge of itself—whether it is in an announcement of a birth or a death, the details of the construction of a new bridge, the problems in the schools, or the heart-warming story of a young boy who risks his life to save his younger sister.

This description shows the newspaper world at its best, and to be a journalist is both exciting and rewarding. It is also hard daily work, in which the high-sounding goals sometimes seem to be totally forgotten. But even in the everyday wear-and-tear of deadlines and rush copy, there is always the special thrill of being where the action is.

Not all newspapers are the big-city dailies that Mr. Sorrells referred to. There are also small newspapers that serve only a special interest, such as organized labor, education, or a political party. These publications usually have a limited circulation, which means they are read by fewer people than newspapers intended for the general public.

Writing ability is basic to success in journalism. Ability to type is essential. Add to these a special desire to serve the common good, acceptance of differences, a warm outlook on humanity, a quick curiosity (to the point of nosiness!), and self-starting discipline. A knowledge of photography helps. So does a good memory and physical stamina—for this is a demanding, fast-paced life.

At the heart of the newspaper is the reporter, the collector of news. In the past, the way to break into reporting was to become a copy boy or girl on a newspaper. The copy boy or girl's job was to carry "copy," or news stories, from the reporter to the editor to the composing room (where type is set), to see that proofs got to the right people, to fetch coffee and sandwiches, and to be generally useful. In between all this, he or she had a chance to read reporters' stories, watch the editor at work, and see how a newspaper was put together. A copy boy or girl could gain considerable experience waiting for the chance to become a cub reporter. Many outstanding journalists began their careers in just this way.

But times have changed. The copy boy or girl can hardly compete with graduates from college schools of journalism. However, rural, small town, and suburban newspapers still continue to hire talented beginners who have no formal training. But editors of large metropolitan dailies prefer applicants with a degree in either journalism or the liberal arts. Editors are also looking more and more for specialists—someone particularly trained to handle news about technical subjects, about politics, education, science, or military developments.

Reporters are not limited to newspapers. Reporters for wire services like United Press International and the Associated Press, write on-the-spot news from central locations—usually large cities or capital cities—and send their stories to newspapers all over the world by teletype, transoceanic cable, or radio. Reporters also cover news for radio and television in such jobs as roving reporters, teletype editors, and reporter-announcers. National news magazines, such as *Time* or *Newsweek,* grab the top professional reporters with years of experience in journalism. "Stringers" are reporters who cover local news for a newspaper and are paid, not on a straight salary, but on the basis of the number of stories printed. Sometimes a reporter for a city daily will serve as a stringer for a national news magazine.

Back to the ranch! The positions of newspaper editors are usually filled from the ranks of those already employed by the paper. Editors generally have many years of reporting experience.

The editor's job is to assign stories to be covered by reporters, evaluate and edit (that is, make changes when necessary) the work of reporters, plan layout of the news, write headlines, and mark copy for the printer indicating size and kind of type. On a small newspaper the editor will do almost anything and everything—sometimes even going out to cover a story. A large city newspaper will most likely have these editorial positions:

Managing editor: Generally supervises all news coverage, planning, and presentation of news.

City editor: Assigns reporters and photographers, edits stories of city and suburban news, marks copy for printer, and decides on news layout.

National editor: Handles news of national scope from the Washington Press Bureau and the wire services (AP, UPI). (A foreign editor may handle overseas news. Or a "wire editor" may handle both national and foreign news.)

Sports editor: Responsible for sports coverage and pictures and the layout of the sports page. Possibly writes a sports column.

Family life editor: Deals with human interest stories, cultural events, society and club news, and consumer and homemaking news.

*Family life editors and reporters cover events such as fashion
shows.*

Other possible editors include picture editor, rewrite editor, make-up editor, business and finance editor, religious editor, arts (music, arts, books) editor, and political editor. On smaller newspapers each of these jobs may be done by a reporter-editor, or several jobs may be combined into one.

On magazines, editorial positions are likely to include editor-in-chief, managing editor, fiction editor, article editor, and special departments editors. Magazine staff writers, like news reporters, work on a salary basis and write stories on assignment. Free-lance material comes in by mail, from writers and literary agents.

In the newspaper advertising department, which is completely separate from the editorial department and has its own staff, the chief writing position is that of the copy writer. A copy writer works from a layout, which is a hand-drawn plan of a proposed advertisement and is made by a layout artist. On the layout, the artist roughly sketches in the merchandise to be advertised, and then with straight lines shows where the advertising copy will go. The copy writer then writes copy to fit exactly into the lines indicated by the layout.

Large stores prepare their own advertisements and have their own advertising departments. Many businesses hire advertising agencies to handle their work. Copy writers can find employment at newspapers, magazines, retail stores, and advertising agencies.

Copy writers need a flair for words, just as do reporters. College journalism departments teach courses in advertising, and most topflight executives in advertising have college degrees. But many an excellent copy writer is one who has not only mastered the technique of writing copy, but also has had a lot of experience in plain living.

One retail advertising manager said that his best copy writer was a woman who had no formal training but was a "whiz with words." She had also bought an old house and remodeled it, she drove a secondhand car that often needed repairs, she had raised a family of two boys and one girl, and she could fix the plumbing if she had to.

"She writes outstanding retail advertising copy," he said. "She knows from experience just exactly what people want to find out about merchandise—whether it is kitchenware, baby clothes, boys' corduroy pants, or the shingles for the roof of the house! She could not have learned all that from a book. Her copy is bright and clever—but at the same time, it is down to earth."

Cobol...Fortran...PL 1...Algol

A technical writer says, "We write not only to be understood — but in such a way that we cannot be misunderstood."

IF THE TITLE of this chapter looks like Greek to you, do not be alarmed. You are not alone. Those terms just happen to be the names of four computer languages, those artificially produced languages that have their very own grammar, word arrangement, and dictionary—the only kind a computer can understand.

In the modern world, discoveries in science and technology are big business. As a result, business and industry are using more and more writers with some technical knowledge—both to write *for* business and industry and to write *about* business and industry. These writers can be divided into two groups: the trade writers and the technical writers. Each classification contains both salaried and free-lance writers.

THE TRADE WRITER

Trade magazines are a wide open field for writers. Since their editors are not constantly working their way

If you want to communicate with a computer, you have to "speak its language."

through mountains of manuscripts, as editors of general interest magazines do, the competition is not as keen. In fact, sometimes the editors of trade magazines do not get enough material to fill their publications. Payment for material is not as high as elsewhere, but a writer who wants to break into nonfiction will find this a good field in which to start.

No matter what a writer's interests, education, background, or job, he or she can find a trade publication to match. The readers range from bakers to electricians to atomic scientists to hardware clerks! Some magazines come out monthly, others quarterly. Altogether, they buy some five thousand articles a month.

You do not have to be a whiz at technology, but if you are writing for bakers, it helps to know something about baking. Most articles are just a matter of careful, accurate reporting. These magazines exist only to supply their readers with ideas, enthusiasm, new-products information, contacts, data—anything that might be useful to a person working in a particular trade. The editors and staff writers for trade magazines have full-time, salaried jobs.

Also in the category of trade writers for business and industry are the editors and writers of "house organs," those company-produced magazines and newspapers.

Every large industry has its own house publication. Altogether, there are six thousand of them. Most house organs are staff-written—that is, written by people salaried for that purpose.

THE TECHNICAL WRITER

Technical writers combine their ability with words with a good grasp of some specialized field, such as engineering, mechanics, electricity, medicine, or agriculture. A technical writer is not necessarily a specialist in the field, but he or she knows it well enough to understand both its technical vocabulary and its jargon, or slang. The technical writer can put all this terminology into language that can be understood by people who have no special knowledge of the field. Technical writing, then, requires both the ability to write and an understanding of the technical subject. For this reason, qualified writers are scarce, and salaries are excellent.

Technical writing jobs are found mostly with companies that conduct research and also make products to fit very specific needs of certain customers. They seek out the special needs of these customers and even suggest such needs to them. These companies handle many government contracts for research and development in communications, military weapons, and aircraft.

Within this framework, the technical writer works in these three main categories:

Writing the technical proposal. The company presents a proposal to a customer who has shown some interest in a new development or idea, or a new product. The proposal is a "selling" proposition that brings together all the information from many engineers, the management, and the technical writers. A proposal may be fifty pages long, or it may be a hundred. One technical writer told of just completing a seventeen-volume proposal for his company, which manufactures military aircraft. Millions of dollars of business can depend on how effectively a writer presents this proposal.

Writing the technical report. If a proposal is successful, the customer will want progress reports on product

Learning electronics in the air force by following a clearly written instruction manual.

development. Since the report must give a favorable image of the company to the customer, the writer is doing a public relations job as well as a technical job. The proposal deals with future possibilities, while the technical report deals with past events.

Writing handbooks and instruction material. Manuals need to be written to instruct customers how to operate and take care of an industry's products—whether these products be air conditioners, power tools, or toys. Anyone who has struggled with the "simple" directions on how to assemble a child's toy knows the frustrations that can result from poorly worded instructions. Imagine, then, the disaster of badly worded manuals on the operation of spacecraft or military equipment!

Computers have opened up a new direction for technical writers. The aim in the computer field is to help solve "information-handling" problems in areas as varied as the diagnosis of disease and urban development. Writers search out the facts by feeding information into computers, analyzing the findings, and then writing clear, accurate descriptions for their computer customers. Most writers in this new area of technical writing are trained for their jobs at company expense, often at full pay.

Medical writers serve doctors and researchers in much the same way as a technical writer serves engineers. They translate medical findings into understandable language, for papers to be delivered at conventions, material for books, or articles for medical journals.

Small Paragraphs about Big Jobs

"Do not fail to be a novice in the beginning, because all doing comes from learning."

—Erskine Caldwell

RUSS WAS A FELLOW who liked to make up new words. One of his favorites was "glom," a shortened version of "agglomerate"—which means "to gather together in a mass." So, a la Russ, this chapter will "glom" together varied writing careers—each of which offers open-ended opportunity and challenge.

WRITERS IN POLITICS AND GOVERNMENT

Every political candidate running for office wants to win. This goal can be achieved only by convincing the voters that he or she is their best choice. Words are the politician's most useful tool.

The primary function of the political campaign writer is to supply the candidate with the right words. He or she does this by writing speeches, campaign literature, and handouts and by translating political platforms into words that the general public can understand. He or she also writes press releases (news stories) that put the candidate in a good light. For the political writer, newspaper experience is a big plus. So is a general political background—knowledge of political party people and party positions—on both sides of the political fence.

A job possibility in government is legislative research. State legislatures often hire research-writers, who dig up all the facts about the bills that they must vote on. The writers then write up this information in a readable, well-organized form for the legislators to use. A legislative researcher may work for one political party, or if paid by the state, for all parties.

Government officials of some status such as governors and mayors may have their own publicity or public relations person to handle news and write press releases. Cities and counties also hire public relations people to attract new business and industry, to write up news on developments, and to work on tourist information.

On the federal level, senators, congressional representatives, and, of course, the president and vice-president, have assistants whose main job is to write speeches, meet with reporters, and keep their home territories informed of their Washington activities. These writing positions usually go to men and women who are experienced in both politics and journalism. A beginner does well to work on the local level—for an alderman for example, or state legislator—where his or her efforts will be truly appreciated and used.

Civil service examinations open the door to many government writing positions. Open competitive examinations are held for "informational writers." Those who pass the test become eligible for placement in such departments as highways, corrections, education, or business development. Although these examinations can be taken by high school graduates, a college education is desirable. Separate tests are given for technical writers.

EDUCATIONAL WRITING

Schools today are recognizing the need for professional writing help. Modern education uses a variety of materials that need to be written and written well: study guides, film strip commentaries, course outlines, guides for parents, newsletters, and faculty handbooks. Also, the writing of applications for federal and private money grants has become an important part of modern education. Composing these applications is a vast writing project. Some institutions have full-time project writers; others hire educational writers on a project-to-project basis.

FINANCIAL WRITING

An author who has specialized in this field says that it is "sadly in need of good writing." He suggests that writers find some area of special interest to them and then specialize in it. Such areas could be metals (gold or silver, for instance), banking, stock brokerage, international trade, or aerospace.

Financial writing deals with facts, not opinions. A writer need not be an economic genius (it would help!) but a good business, economics, or financial background gives the beginner a head start. The research itself is an education, and through it a writer will build a specialty.

TRAVEL WRITING

Modern travel editors like articles with some fresh angle—a news "peg" that can tie the article to some

Updating an aircraft maintenance manual. Changes are distributed throughout the world on 16mm microfilm.

current event—or a clever slant. Often a travel article can be found in your own backyard—perhaps a historical landmark, a state park, or some unusual resort that would make for a good family holiday. You can try your hand at travel writing by doing stories about summer camp, a family vacation, or even a Sunday drive. These stories will be nice mementos even if they are not published. General rule: be enthusiastic—but do not gush!

BOOKLET EDITING
Pamphlets and booklets are put out by industries, professional associations, government agencies, and civic and religious organizations. (You may have to do a free one to get a foothold here.) A writer-editor who takes on the whole responsibility of a booklet must be prepared to do research, interview, and attend committee meetings—as well as write the copy, plan the layout, and arrange for printing. Extra bonus: Research often provides enough material for a nonfiction article on the side.

PUBLICITY AND PUBLIC RELATIONS
Writers in these fields are known as "public relations people" or press agents. They handle news for their clients, who may be anyone—a movie star, a bestselling author, or a politician—who wants to keep his or her name in the public eye. They also work on fundraising campaigns for political parties, charities, and churches. They may be hired for almost any project that needs publicity—a new movie, a new product, or a new shopping center.

Some companies have full-time public relations people; others keep one on a part-time "retainer" (a small monthly fee, whether he or she works or not). For special events, payment is usually on a flat fee basis or on an hourly rate. Here again, the best way to begin is as a volunteer, usually free, for some organization. Working on publicity for a Scout pancake breakfast or a Little League tournament might be a fun way for a young writer to get a start in public relations. Learn how to write news and how to develop publicity angles. This is a creative, exciting type of writing—and lots of hard work.

PHOTOJOURNALISM

A picture may say more than a thousand words, but combine pictures and words—and the combination really talks! About 50 percent of all photographs are supported by some kind of writing.

There are two ways to start in photojournalism: take a chance and shoot a picture-story and hope to sell it, or come up with such an interesting idea that some editor will give the "go ahead." Be sure to take samples of your photography along with your terrific idea.

A young person interested in photojournalism might work up a picture story on a favorite pet, a younger sister, or a vacation. What a nice letter to an out-of-town grandmother or a pen pal!

Beginners will do well to start with newspapers, dailies, or Sunday editions. Many a successful photojournalist started with the school newspaper.

A good camera and lots of enthusiasm are essential to success in this field.

From Rumpelstiltskin to Dr. Seuss

"Children hunger for plot . . . They abhor chaos — unless, of course, they are creating it themselves."
—Edward Fenton

IF ANY YOUNG author has the notion that writing for children is easy, banish the thought. Do not get caught with the false notion that if you cannot make the grade in the adult field, you can always write for the juvenile market. That approach is a perfect guarantee of failure.

Juvenile fiction and nonfiction is a very special field with high standards. As one writer states it: "Adults will put up with a slow beginning, a meandering plot. But not so with children. They demand that writing be vivid and true."

Children want plot, they want order. Stories must be believable; characters and endings must ring true. But at the same time, children can soar with fantasy as no adult can! They want a lively pace, a sense of going somewhere. They expect a book to hold their interest.

If it does not, they will not hesitate to slam it shut!

Wordage, too, is limited, both in books and magazines. Authors who cannot tell a tale inside set limits have their manuscripts returned to be shortened—if they are lucky!

Lee Wyndham, who is the author of almost fifty children's books and more than two hundred short stories, suggests that beginning writers start with children's stories, rather than books. She says that a writer learns in stories how to plot, how to write at a brisk pace, and how to write without wasting words.

Children's magazine markets can be divided into two large groupings: the general interest magazines, such as *Jack and Jill, Boys' Life,* and *Young Miss,* and the religious magazines. Sometimes a story may fit either market. Religious magazines, however, generally expect a story to teach some moral principle (but you better not preach!), while the general magazine may use pure entertainment material.

In age groupings, magazines may be divided into the small fry (ages five to nine), elementary and junior high (nine to thirteen), and the high school group (thirteen to seventeen).

In the book market, publishers have somewhat similar divisions. It is well for a beginning writer to study a large number of books in the age group he or she would like to write for. Here are the main groupings:

Picture Books (ages two to five). Here pictures tell as much of the story as do the words. Adults read these books to children. Some publishers like art suggestions; others prefer just the text. Do not send drawings unless you are a professional artist. Editors usually arrange for the artwork.

Picture Story Books (ages six to nine). Most of these are still read to children by adults, so words do not need to be extremely simple. Plot is increasingly important.

Easy-to-Read Books (ages six to nine). These are books designed for grades 1, 2, and 3, where children are beginning to read for themselves. Vocabulary and sentence structure are simple, but there must be enough story to keep the reader's interest. Not easy to do!

The Eight-to-Twelve Group. This is the in-between stage—the biggest and most avid reading category. The readers in this group are not yet teenagers, but they have left easy books far behind. Plot, action, mystery, sport, biography—everything interests them. A slight division begins here into boys' and girls' books, but the use of both sexes in a book makes for good general reading.

The Teenage Group (older than twelve years). One usually thinks of teenagers as thirteen to sixteen, but in the reader-group, they could be from age ten on up, depending on the individual's reading level. By age sixteen, good readers are reading adult books, so perhaps fifteen is a practical top-age limit. There is much more separation into boys' books and girls' books. The books deal with teenage problems and feature characters that teenagers can identify with. Adults have only minor roles.

Is the juvenile field a financially attractive one for a writer? It can be. Magazine payments are not as high as in the adult field, so a writer's output has to be large and constant. But the market is broad and always in need of material.

In the book field, an author may do as well, or even better, with a juvenile novel as an adult one. The publication of the juvenile book will not be a splashy affair —there will be no autographing parties and very little publicity. But long after an adult novel may be out of print, a well-written juvenile book may still be selling steadily. One writer has said that his juvenile mysteries kept him in bread and butter while he worked on his adult novel. Many writers in this field, however, have other jobs to supplement their income.

But juvenile writers have many other rewards for their labors. No reading public is more faithful to a preferred author. As any parent or older child in a family knows, the favorite picture book is truly beloved. A young child never tires of it. In fact, it is read and read and read—until the covers and pages fall apart!

And the author's day is often brightened by letters such as this one: "I really loved your book, *The Secret of Willow Coulee.* It was so exciting. Especially where Benjy got thrown in the river. And almost drowned. That was neat! It's the best book I've *ever* read in a long time."

Can an author ask for more?

Penny-Pinching,
Patience, and Prestige

"The theatre is so extraordinarily visual . . ."
—Truman Capote

A WELL-KNOWN WRITER and literary critic once told a group of young playwrights that in order to succeed they had to dare to be poor and patient.

To have a long-running play on Broadway is the same as having a novel on the bestseller list for months on end. Both are achievements that a writer can aim for, but not all plays and not all novels are destined for that kind of fame or fortune. Yet what greater thrill can a playwright have than to see his or her imagined people come to life on a stage—be it in a Broadway hit or in the class play at Central High School!

Hundreds of plays are written and published for amateur use—for high schools, church groups, and drama clubs. A beginner would do well to try writing this kind of play. Here one can learn both the possibilities and the limits of the dramatic medium, the stage.

Unlike short stories and novels, which the reader sees only in the mind, the play is completely visual—and it happens now. The events take place right there in front of the eyes of the audience. And all the plot and character development must be achieved through sight, action, and dialogue. Again, this is unlike the novel and short story where the author can describe not only places and people, but the characters' thoughts and feelings. No wonder a play is difficult to write!

Plays for amateurs have strict requirements, somewhat like those in children's literature. Characters must be wholesome and believable, and themes should be worthwhile. There should be between eight and fifteen characters in the cast, and multi-star leading roles are preferred over one main character. All major characters are introduced in the first third of the play. Important events happen on the stage—not off of it.

In spite of the strict standards, these plays need not be pablum. Important problems facing today's young people can be used for the theme: problems of conscience, education, or world conflict; love and young marriage; and relations with parents. There is drama everywhere for an aspiring young playwright!

Television is a monster that devours dramatic material at a rate never before experienced. A beginner's best hope of breaking into television writing is by getting a job—any job—in the television industry. Many television writers were once studio workers, publicity writers, or actors. The transition into writing is made easier, not only by the contacts made on the job, but also by a practical knowledge of what a television drama requires. Educational television is a good training ground and often welcomes volunteer help.

Screenwriting for motion pictures is another specialized drama field. The screenplay is much like any other play except that the scenes are shorter and more directions are given. Action is outlined in considerable detail, and some camera positions are indicated. Screenplays may be adapted from a novel, short story, stage play, or even nonfiction material. Only about 25 percent of all screenplays are originals written for the movies.

Formerly, each major movie studio had a large reading department. This department's job was to search for good screenplay material. Now, however, reading departments have all but vanished.

Then how is material for screenplays discovered? Best-seller novels and hit plays are a big source, and literary agents another. Producers, directors, and even stars are on the lookout for something new and different.

To sell an original play to a Broadway or movie producer is very difficult without an agent. And, as was pointed out in other chapters, an agent is looking for the professional, proved writer, not for the amateur. However, many agents who handle plays will read material if a query letter convinces them that the writer has something worthwhile to offer.

Opportunities for playwrights have increased in recent years. A great many college and community theaters are receiving outright grants of money, and as a consequence they are able to produce original work.

Producers' advice to young playwrights seems to be unanimous. They say:

- Get the best education you can. Take course work in theater arts in some college. If possible, work for a degree in theater arts.

- Find a "little theater" and work in it.

- Work on production—settings, lighting, sound, and costumes. This will help you write a play out of knowledge of the stage itself.

- Submit your play for production to a high school, college, or community theater, and if possible, work with the actors who put it on.

- Then—with some experience and "credits" under your belt, approach a literary agent to handle your work. Now you have something concrete to offer.

To go or not to go to New York? Some say, "Yes."

Others cry loudly, "No!" A well-known agent exclaimed, "It does not matter one whit where a writer lives. I can sell a good play if the author lives in Timbuktu!"

Rhyme, Rhythm, and Reason

"A poem is imagination's child . . . it makes the invisible visible . . ."
—Ruth Slonim

JUDSON JEROME, poet and critic, once described poetry as the "most over-produced commodity in the world." And, he pointed out, there is a very small market for all that production.

Does this discouraging state of affairs stop the poet? It does not. Nor should it. Every writer must write what he or she feels—regardless of how many, or how few, are writing in the same field, and even if the prospect of publication is dim.

However, it would be unrealistic for a young person to decide to make poetry a career in the same way he or she would choose law or business administration. For there are hardly any full-time poets, and none who make a solid living by writing poetry. As George P. Elliott said in an interview in *Writer's Digest,* the poet must either work for a living or live in poverty. The thing for the poet to do, however, is to find a job that will not interfere with the writing of poetry.

Poet Pablo Neruda at work.

A large number of poets have academic professions—they are teachers or professors; some are "poets-in-residence" at universities. Others are writers, business people, and farmers—even politicians. Writing poetry can be a satisfying hobby, but a poet had better plan to get bread and butter by some more dependable means.

One successful writer figured it out this way: If a poet could keep some fifty or sixty poems constantly in the mail, both to large general interest magazines and to the small journals or poetry magazines, he or she could expect from ten to fifteen sales a year. The "pay" for many of these would be in complimentary contributor's copies of the magazine that published the poem. Others might bring from ten to fifty dollars each, if the poet is lucky.

Economic returns from poetry books (usually published only by established poets) are small compared to the money earned by other types of books. Having a poem included in a collection of poems may bring in some additional money. Total all this—it does not make for a very impressive annual income.

Markets for poetry include the general magazines, women's magazines, juvenile publications, poetry journals, "little magazines," literary quarterlies and reviews, some newspapers, and book publishers. Light verse, or humorous verse, is often used as a filler in many magazines; some magazines have full humor pages.

Those who enjoy rhyme and rhythmic play on words, and are clever with turning a phrase and an idea, can find a market in selling verse to greeting card companies. Payment here is by line or, as for studio cards, by idea.

Reflections on
Rejections and Dejections

". . . climb those mountains. Don't make them out of molehills."
—B. J. Chute

A WRITER PROBABLY dreads these two things more than anything else: the rejection slip and the writer's block. Yet to remain a writer, one must accept the fact that both are as certain to come as night and rainfall. And they can be just as useful.

Rejection slips are those unhappy slips of paper that inform a writer that his or her manuscript just did not make the grade at such-and-such a magazine or publishing house. They are always a blow to the author. No matter how many rejections you have received in the past, you are never quite ready for the next one! For each manuscript leaves its author's hands with great hopes attached.

Editors reject a manuscript for many reasons. Some of these reasons have to do with the manuscript itself: the writing may be poor, the plot slight, the characters not fully developed, the theme trivial or nonexistent, the research inadequate, the idea stale—just to suggest a few possibilities. Or the reasons may have very little to do with the writing at all: the publishing house may be overstocked with this type of material; it may have recently purchased a similar piece of work; or it may not even be in the market for this particular kind of manuscript.

Rejection slips come in many shapes and sizes—each bearing its own kind of discouragement or encouragement. For instance:

● The printed "form" letter (the kind they have in ready-made stacks in the publishing house). Alas! The worst type (other than no rejection slip at all). Cold and impersonal as ice. Discouragement indeed!

● The printed "form" letter—but what is here at the bottom? Some kind soul has pencilled a note. "Sorry, but do try us again." That is encouragement!

● The personal letter with inadequate statements such as: "does not suit our present needs," or "does not fit our list." That is puzzlement! For what does it really mean? Who knows? The poor author can only try reading between the lines.

● The personal letter with the real reason for rejection. Something meaningful like: "This is a well-conceived story but the ending does not seem real. Could Ann resolve her problem in some more convincing way?" Happy is the author who gets one of these! Encouragement, of course! The editor would not bother to write unless you had stirred some interest. And if you rewrote this manuscript, the editor just might like to see it again—even though he or she does not say so directly.

Rejections are not, of course, limited to writers only. Everyone suffers from rejections of some sort—the girl who doesn't make the swimming team; the boy whose science project is unacceptable for extra credit; the contractor who bids for the job that is awarded to a competitor; the college graduate who applies for admission to law school and is turned down.

In order to benefit from mistakes and failures, each person must learn to make rejection fruitful. One author's philosophy is, "All things negative become positive—*if you just keep growing.*" Of no effort are those words more true than of failure in writing. Writers who ask themselves honestly, "Why did this manuscript get turned down? What did I do wrong? How can I improve it?"—these writers are on their way to learning from their errors.

Writers, if they are to survive, must learn the hard discipline of failure. One writer said (ten years later) of a book of hers that no one would publish, "I'm glad now that it was rejected. I had not realized then what a bad piece of writing it was. I am glad it is not in print." Failure, like experience, is a rough teacher who spares no blows. One of the prime requisites of a writer, some say, is a thick skin. But not too thick! Writers need to be sensitive. Rejections should make them determined to write better, to write more precisely, to think more clearly, and to search for originality and depth of meaning. When that happens, rejections have served a good purpose, no matter how difficult it may be for a writer to admit it!

Rejections, however, are not all tears and wailing. There is always a funny side, and every author has his or her favorite rejection story. A well-known novelist shared this rejection story with a writer's group:

As a regular contributor to two competitive love story magazines, in the days when such "pulp" magazines were popular, she had agreed to write one story a month for each of these magazines. One month, to her dismay, both magazines rejected the stories she had sent to them. Wrote one editor, "We are sorry, but this is not up to your usual standard." Said the other, "Compared to your former work, this one leaves us a little cold."

Undaunted, the author switched stories and envelopes and sent them out again the same day. In a week came the first check with a note: "This one has just the kind of emotional warmth we are looking for." A few days later came the second acceptance. "You outdid yourself on this one—excellent!" As the saying goes, one editor's food is another editor's poison.

Another writer received a "glowing" rejection. It said, "This is a wonderful story with superb characterizations and fast-moving narrative. We are so sorry we have no room for it." A turndown—but the kind words put the author on cloud nine. Until she looked at the manuscript. Why, it was not hers at all! The story belonged to an author in New Jersey! When she returned the manuscript to her editor, explaining the error, she got her own back promptly by return mail. But with no note at all. She does not know to this day whether those marvelous words of praise were meant for her—or for that man in New Jersey!

For writers, there is always the hope that any rejection is not the final word—that the next one will be an acceptance. The records show that there is ample reason for this optimism.

Consider such famous books as these: *All Quiet on the Western Front, A Tree Grows in Brooklyn, Lust for Life, Anatomy of a Murder*—all were rejected, not once, but several times. When finally published, each went on to become a bestseller. Erskine Caldwell, author of some forty books, write for six whole years without a single acceptance. And incomparable Dr. Seuss had twenty-seven rejections on one of his best books for children.

A long string of rejections, however, can trigger that dreaded disease of authors: the writer's block. Writer's block simply means the inability to write. To a writer this is as tragic as it would be for a swimmer to be thrown into the middle of a lake and discover that he or she could not swim!

Writer's block is very real and is caused by many conditions such as physical or mental ill health, working too long or too hard on one project, emotionally draining experiences (death in the family, divorce, accident), trying to force oneself to write for a market that really does not interest one, and many other reasons.

Writers who have survived these "blocked" stages say it is best not to fight the disease too hard. There are no miracle drugs that work in all cases. Sometimes it pays in the long run to take some time off from the typewriter, to relax, to read, to enjoy other things in life. Sooner or later the ability to write returns.

Students, for instance, know that after studying hard for several hours, one's mind may suddenly go blank. That is the time for a half-hour break, a walk around the block, a ten-minute chat on the phone, or a short nap. Change of pace and rest—whether for a student or a writer—refreshes the mind and spirit and makes both more effective for the next undertaking.

Rejection, dejection, reflection—the ever-present ingredients in a writer's life—they can become either stumbling blocks or building blocks, depending on how honestly and courageously a writer faces them.

How Writers Write

"If you must . . . write."   —Alyce Ingram

IS IT BETTER for an author to write while stretched out on a bed, notebook in hand, scribbling away with a pencil? Or should he or she write standing up, leaning on an old ice box? Laugh if you must, but those are positions which two famous American writers have found to be most creative for them!

Truman Capote, author of *In Cold Blood* and other books, calls himself a "completely horizontal writer." He says he cannot think unless he is lying down, stretched out on a bed or couch, sipping tea or coffee.

In that posture, the first version of his story or chapter is written down, in pencil, in his careful, small upright script. Later he does a complete revision, that too in longhand—and still in bed! The third version he types on a very special kind of yellow paper—and still in bed! He balances his typewriter on his knees and says it works just fine, that he can type up to one hundred words a minute!

Thomas Wolfe, by contrast, was a vertical writer. Terribly restless and over-stimulated when he was working on a book, he would pace back and forth and write standing up, leaning on an old ice box, sometimes banging his head against the wall in dreadful impatience if the thoughts would not stream out of his brain fast enough. He worked feverishly in a cluttered basement apartment, which his editor said looked as though someone had moved in a few hours earlier—and was planning on moving out a few hours later. Thomas Wolfe was a giant genius of a man with a giant hunger to experience everything there was in life. And he wrote the same way—pouring out as many as ten thousand words a day.

Every writer must search out the method of writing that works best for him or her. Most writers agree that actually putting black on white is truly an exhausting physical job. No longer is it enough to have ideas and thoughts in the mind; now they must be put on paper, physically set down in words. As one writer put it: A work of art is work.

Then how to get this work done? What tools are used?

Some writers find the noise of the typewriter distracting, and the hum of an electric one unbearable. They prefer writing in longhand. Others work well directly on a typewriter, especially if they have been trained to compose on a typewriter, as have newspaper reporters.

Some use several tools, as did Mr. Capote. Longhand for first drafts, the typewriter for revisions. Many triple space early drafts—giving themselves plenty of room for additions or changes. One novelist said, "As long as I keep my manuscript on yellow paper, I know it is not finished. When I type it on good white bond paper, I am saying to myself—this is it!" Many modern writers have learned to use the tape recorder, with the words from the tape later put on paper.

Authors often become slaves to their methods and their tools of work. A writer who was stricken with severe arthritis of the hands found she could not think with her mind alone—that she needed her hands at the typewriter to make her brain function at all.

Similarly, Ernest Hemingway is known to have said that his fingers did much of his thinking for him. After an automobile accident, when doctors thought he might lose the use of his right arm, Mr. Hemingway was afraid he would have to stop writing. James Thurber, too, said he had a "sense of thinking" with his fingers. Later when Mr. Thurber's vision became so weak that he could no longer see to use the typewriter, he wrote very little for many years. Finally, with tremendous difficulty, he learned to dictate his stories to a stenographer.

Some writers work at a hectic pace, as did Mr. Wolfe, producing a great deal of wordage, much of which they throw away. Others work laboriously, struggling with each word, writing perhaps a page, or even a paragraph a day. It took Gustave Flaubert a week to write two pages.

Most novels are written in two or three years, but a self-critical perfectionist may take ten years to complete a book. Katherine Ann Porter took twenty years to finish *Ship of Fools*. In contrast, there is the unbelievable Frenchman, George Simenon, who writes his mystery novels in exactly eleven days!

"When I am doing a novel now," says Mr. Simenon, "I do not see anybody. I do not speak to anybody. I do not take a phone call. I live like a monk. All the day, I am one of my characters. I feel what he feels."

After five or six days Mr. Simenon finds the strain almost too much to take. By the eleventh day he is so exhausted that he can work no longer, and that is the reason he must write within this time limit. Before he starts a book, he has his doctor give him a physical check-up—and then he begins. The preliminary work has been simply a matter of putting down the names, ages, and characteristics of his characters. He has no other outline or plan.

Most writers could not work that way. Mr. Capote, for instance, says he has the start, the middle, and the end completely in his mind before he begins to write. Not that he knows exactly *how* he will write them, but he knows where he is headed. Nelson Algren, on the other hand, says that the only way he could finish a book was to "make it longer and longer until something happens—you know, until it finds its own plot—because you cannot outline and fit the thing into it."

However, there are writers who *do* outline, who know precisely what each chapter must say. They say that the outline does not stop their creativity, that their rough plan is still flexible enough for changes and surprises. It does give them a clear sense of direction with a few signposts along the way, so they will not wander too far off the main road.

All writers agree that in order to be a real professional, a writer must work almost every day—and preferably in the same place, a place used only for writing. By sitting in this special spot, the brain seems to click on, the way you would click on a light in a dark hallway.

Herman Wouk, author of *The Caine Mutiny,* says that he tries to write a certain amount each day, five days a week. His work hours are mornings and early afternoons. Victoria Lincoln wakes up way before dawn and writes continually until noon. After lunch she takes a long nap and then rises to write again until dinner time. Arthur Lewis, author of *The Day They Shook the Plum Tree,* says he has a rigid schedule which he never breaks. He writes from 5:30 A.M. to 12:30 P.M. every day—not missing a single day. He both writes and rewrites each morning, so that each day he ends up with "clean copy"—which points to his former newspaper training. Most writers agree that four or five hours a day is good production.

This recital could go on and on. For there are as many methods and schedules as there are writers. What works for one, may not work for another at all. Each freelance writer is his or her own boss—and sometimes not a very good one!

If you should decide to be a writer, you could choose to work only when inspiration fires your mind (but you might not get much written!). Or you might work every day, whether you felt like it or not. Of course, if you chose to go daily to a writing job in some industry or business—from 9 A.M. to 5 P.M.—you need not worry about forcing yourself to follow your own schedule. Or about what the critics will say. Or where to sell your finished writing.

But whether you choose free-lance or a regular writing position—and no matter what your methods or schedules are, your writing will bring you a satisfaction that only another writer can fully understand. For writing —like virtue—is truly its own reward.

Write, Write, Write ...
Read, Read, Read

"The great thing in life is to get yourself right . . . and I found quite early I could only get myself right by writing."
—Henry Green

FOR THIS LAST chapter I am going to switch viewpoints. Now I will use the subjective first-person—the "I". The first-person viewpoint is very personal. I, the author, can talk intimately with you, the reader, as though we were chatting over a coke at the corner drugstore.

A few years ago, a famous novelist advised in *The Writer* magazine that if a person had the desire to write, he or she should try to deny it and try to find some other creative outlet that would be satisfying. He mentioned such alternatives as cooking, sewing, and gardening. After you have done all these, he said, and you still want to write, then write!

I disagreed strongly. The following month I wrote a reply. I asked, Why? Why should a person try to deny the desire to write?

Because the effort to write will not be easy?

Because one's talents may not be enough?

Because one may fail?

We do not say to the aspiring medical student: do everything else first, and then if you still must be a doctor, start your medical education. He or she might, even then, spend years in study and fail the examinations.

Nor do we say to the little fellow impatiently slurring his musical scales, his baseball mitt plunked beside him on the piano bench, "Ah-h, go play your game. What is the use of practicing? You will never give a concert in Carnegie Hall anyway." He most likely will not. But he will have enriched his life in the knowledge and discipline of an art. He will have achieved insights that will help him understand and appreciate the artist who *will* play in Carnegie Hall.

And how about those other creative outlets? Cooking, after all, has its hazards too, and all that comes out of the pot is not worthy of praise. And you might grow more weeds than flowers in your garden.

After all, why should anyone discourage young writers? Why can't we say, instead, in all honesty: Go to it! Write—write—write!

Writing will not be easy. But nothing truly worthwhile is easy. And it is said that writers are never completely happy. That they feel too much. They sense too much. They see how things ought to be—and are not—and they are disturbed. They often write out of pain, out of injustice, out of grief—their own or someone else's. They "feel" for people. Or for animals. For to shape their words, writers must use the raw materials of life, both good and bad, harsh and gentle, ugly and beautiful.

I would say to the young writer: your career may be full of pitfalls and disappointments, frustrations and depressions. But writing will bring you memorable moments of triumph.

Writing will open your eyes to yourself, to the world, to the fascinating creatures that share this planet with you. It will clarify your ideas, and if you let it, it will help you grow as nothing else can. But remember, growth is always painful. Growth means moving from safe and familiar grounds to the unsafe and unguaranteed. It is much easier to deny growth or to avoid it, but for this you will pay an even dearer price later on.

So go to it! If you want to be a writer, plan for your writing career. Learn, first of all, to master grammar, punctuation, and the construction of sentences and paragraphs. Whether you go into advertising, business, technical or creative writing, you will need this knowledge. Master these fundamentals so well that you will not have to think about them when you write, that you will use them correctly in an automatic way. This mastery will save you more headaches than you can imagine.

If you plan to go into trade or technical writing, put a little extra mental "elbow grease" into your math and your sciences. These are your stepping stones.

Combining your writing with thorough knowledge in some other area might lead you into careers that combine two fields, such as agricultural journalist, home economics writer, foods editor, fashion reporter, science writer, or political analyst.

And learn to read. Learn to read not only as a *reader*

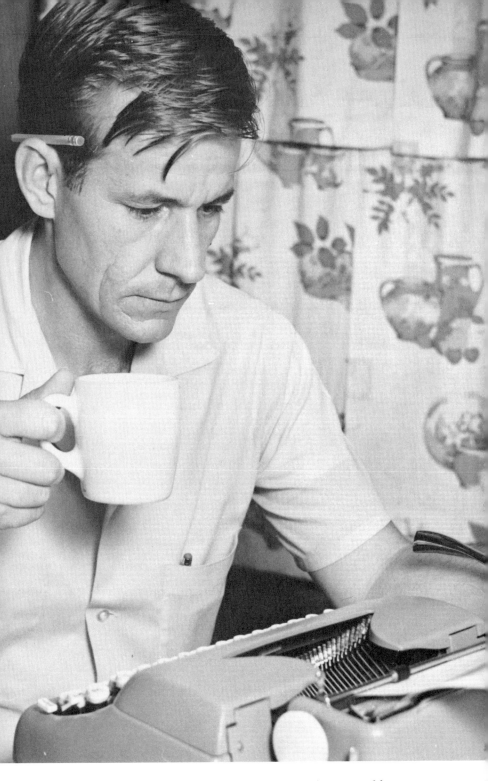

Writing is work, but it is also the source of memorable moments of triumph!

but as a *writer*. Read first for meaning and understanding; then go back and study *how* the writer used the language in order to create the effect he or she wanted.

Learn to look at the shape of words on a page. Did you notice how I used three questions as though each were a paragraph at the beginning of this chapter? I did this to gain special emphasis—not only by what the question asked, but by how it appeared on the page.

Read everything. Read the breakfast cereal box—it is a lesson in advertising! Read the political handouts in a campaign—notice how the copy writer used pictures and text effectively (or ineffectively). Analyze them: do they try to say too much (usually!) or too little? Read direct mail advertising just to see the variety of gimmicks employed to capture attention. Study one of your school books—notice how it is laid out, for clarity, or logical use. Read the billboards. See how a few words are used to give a message to someone traveling at fifty miles per hour.

There are lessons in writing all around you. A writer reads to find out *what* the words say—but also *how* the message was accomplished.

Start a newspaper or literary magazine at your school, or write a play and have your friends help you put it on. Try to write a poem or story for a magazine you read and send it to the publisher. Later on, take classes in journalism or debate; both teach you how to organize your mind. Consider English themes and book reports a special challenge.

Do not confine your reading to just one level, or to one field. Expand your mind so it can eventually make the leap from the Hardy Boys to James Joyce's *Ulysses*. Read sometimes in areas which are totally unfamiliar to you, even areas you dislike. Construct your "window on the world" so it has width and breadth—make it a big window, a picture window, or a corner window so you can see in many different directions. Then choose the direction that is right for you.

So my final bit of advice to young writers is this: Do not deny the desire. Do not search for alternatives. Live. Write. Experiment. Write. Cook, garden, sew, raise a family. But write, write, write!

Writing is not something apart from living. It is the same thing—plus. You simply go one step farther. You put it on paper. You rearrange it. You test its values. You communicate it.

As novelist Ernest Hemingway said, you have to live to know your subject, and then you have to learn how to write—and each of these takes a lifetime to learn.

So why should we—who want to be writers—waste our time looking for alternatives? We should not! We should set sail today!

Bon voyage!

For More Information

The Writer and *Writer's Digest* are monthly magazines that feature articles on how to write effectively for publication. The following books are also good sources of information.

Foster, Joanna. *Pages, Pictures, and Print: A Book in the Making.* New York: Harcourt, Brace, Jovanovich, 1958.

Goldreich, Gloria and Esther. *What Can She Be? A Newscaster.* New York: Lothrop, Lee & Shepard, 1973.

Grumich, Charles A., ed. *Reporting/Writing from Front Row Seats.* New York: Simon & Schuster, 1971.

Haeberle, Billi. *Looking Forward to a Career: Radio and Television.* Minneapolis: Dillon Press, 1974.

Larranaga, Bob. *Looking Forward to a Career: Advertising.* Minneapolis: Dillon Press, 1973.

Yolen, Jane H. *Writing Books for Children.* Boston: The Writer, 1973.

Index

Ethel Tigue first had a poem published at age twelve, and has been writing ever since. She was editor of the college newspaper at the University of Minnesota in Duluth; a reporter for the *Wilmington Star,* Wilmington, North Carolina; and city editor of *Women's News,* a Duluth weekly newspaper.

Mrs. Tigue later went into advertising, beginning as a copywriter and working her way up to advertising manager of the Duluth Glass Block, a large department store. She has freelanced in advertising and magazine layout, directed a writers' workshop in St. Paul, Minnesota, and taught both junior and senior high school.

During the years, she has written short stories, articles, poems, and book reviews. She is the author of *Betrayal,* an adult novel; co-author with Louise Bower of two juvenile novels, *Packy* and *The Secret of Willow Coulee;* and winner of the $1,000 McKnight Foundation Humanities Award for the novel.